One Dive in C

-: Authors :-

Ms. Nehal Dave

Ms. Miral Kothari   Ms. Ripal Ranpara

ISBN-13: 978-1723117503
Title ID: 8815723

Contents

Acknowledgement

We would like to express our gratitude to the many people who saw us through this book; to all those who provided support and offered comments.

We would like to give special thanks to the Honourable Secretary P.P. Sadhu Tyagvallabhdas of Yogidham Gurukul for his continuous shower of blessings.

We also take this opportunity to thank the Principal Shree M. & N. Virani Science College Dr. K. D. Ladva for their guidance and support.

We also thank to Head of computer science department Dr. Stavan Patel and Dr. Hitendra Donga for their motivational support.

We would like to thank our family members who supported and encouraged us all the time.

Last but not the least: We beg forgiveness of all those who have been with us over the journey and whose names we have failed to mention.

Introduction to C

Communication:

A language is the method or medium of human communication either spoken or written. To exchange information from one person to another is known as communication which can be done using any language. One condition is there that a common language should be there for a proper communication. If a common language is not there then we require one mediator to translate the content.

Computer Language:

When communication between two persons is there then they must have one common language as we know. If we wish to communicate with a computer then we need one language which is known to both which is not possible. So we require one language through which we can give instructions to computer which is known as computer language. In short we can say that a language which helps a human to communicate with a computer is known as computer language. Any person can communicate with a computer via programs. These programs are created in a specific language which is known as programming language. Some examples of computer languages are C, C++, Java etc.

About C Language:

C language is developed at Bell Laboratories in 1972 by Dennis Ritchie. The C language is a structure oriented programming language. Structured oriented means large programs are divided into small programs called functions. C language follows "top-down" approach. It is used to develop portable applications. Some keywords are main, if, for, while, switch, do while, break etc. are used to create C program.

C Character Set:

It includes alphabets, digits and special symbol as a character. Using these characters in different combination we can create variables. With the help of variables, keywords, operators etc. we can create a program. So we can say that character set is a row material to create any program.

Character sets have main two categories.

1. Source character set
   a . Alphabets
      o A to Z OR a to z
   b . Digits
      o 0 to 9

   c . Special characters
      o % percent sign,

- o <   less than,
- o (left parenthesis,
- o {   left flower brace etc.

d. Space
- o \b   blank space,
- o \n   new line,
- o \t   horizontal tab   etc.

2. Execution character set
    a. Escape sequence or Backslash characters

Escape Sequence	Usage
'\a'	Beep from cpu
'\b'	Back space
'\n'	New line
'\t'	Horizontal tab
'\''	Single quote
'\"'	Double quote
'\?'	Question mark
'\\'	Backslash
'\0'	Null

Example:

```
#include<stdio.h>
#include<conio.h>
main()
{
    clrscr();
        printf("\n\n \t\t\t \"Hello \" ");
    getch();
}
```

C-Tokens:

The smallest unit which is used to develop C program is called C tokens. There are six types of tokens available in C. List of C tokens are as below.

1. Identifiers
2. Keywords
3. Constants
4. Strings
5. Special characters
6. Operators

1. Identifiers:

Identifiers are created by the programmer using combination of character set.

Example : name of variables, functions, arrays, etc.

2. Keywords:

Keywords are special words that are used to in program. Any keyword is not used as a variable name and constant name.

Example: int, float, main etc.

3. Constant:

Constant means a fixed value defined to the variable which cannot be changed during the execution of the program.

Example: 10, 'a', "hello" etc.

4. Strings:

String is a collection characters.

Example: "hello"

5. Special characters

Any character which is not an alphabet or not a digit is known as special character.

Example: #, %, & etc.

6. Operators

A symbol of a word which is used to perform some specific operation is known as operator. There are different types of operators available in c as per the task.

Example: arithmetic operators (+, -, *, /, %), logical operators (&&, | |,!) etc.

Symbolic Constant

Symbolic constants are also known as constant variables or macro. When a fix value is required which will not be changed during into the program at that time symbolic constants are used.

Advantages

A program will be easier and powerful. If requirement of changing a value is there then by fewer modifications we will have our program ready.

Syntax:

```
#define   symbolic-name   value of constants
```

Example :

```
#define PI 3.14159
#define AGE 18
#include<stdio.h>
#define PI 3.14
main()
  {
        int r=5;
        float a;
        a = PI * r * r;
        printf("Area of circle = %f",a);
        getch();
  }
```

Operators

An operator is a symbol which is used to perform either a calculative task or logical task. Different types of operators available in C which are as follows:

1. Arithmetic operators.
2. Relational operators.
3. Logical operators.
4. Assignment operators.
5. Conditional operators.
6. Bitwise operators.
7. Sizeof operators.

1) Arithmetic Operators:

Arithmetic operators are used to do arithmetic operations. Arithmetic operators are classified into two categories.

1. Unary Operators:

These operators are used with single operands.

Operator	Use of operator
++	Increases a value by one
--	Decreases a value by one

11

Example

```
#include<stdio.h>
void main()
{
  int i;
        for(i=1;i<=5;i++)
        {
                printf("\n %d",i);
        }
}
```

2. Binary operators:

Operator	Use of operator
+	Adds two operands
-	Subtract two operands
*	Multiply two operands
/	Divide two operands
%	Remainder from division

Example

```
#include<stdio.h>
void main()
{
  int a, b,sum=0;
       printf("\nEnter two nos : ");
       scanf("%d %d", &a, &b);
            sum= a + b;
       printf("Sum : %d", sum);
}
```

2) Relational Operators:

Relational operators are utilized to do comparison between variables.

Operator	Use of operator
>	Greater than
>=	Greater than or equal to
<	Less than
<=	Less than or equal to
==	Equal to
!=	Not equal to

Example

```c
#include <stdio.h>
void main()
{
        int a,b;
        printf("Enter two numbers: ");
        scanf("%d ",&a);

        printf("Enter two numbers: ");
        scanf("%d ",&b);

        if(a>b)
        {
                printf("%d is maximum",a);
        }
         else
        {
                printf("%d is maximum",b);
        }
}
```

3) Logical Operators :

Logical operators are used when we have multiple conditions to check. a logical operator is a boolean value either true or false.

Operator	Name	Use of operator
&&	Logical and	Returns true if both conditions are true
||	Logical or	Returns true if any one condition is true
!	Logical not	Returns true if the operand is 0

```c
#include <stdio.h>
void main()
{
  int a=10,b=20;
      if (a>b && a !=0)
        {
            printf("\n both conditions are true");
      }
}
```

Assignment Operator

Assignment operators are also known as shorthand operators. Assignment operators are used to assign value to a variable.

Operator	Use of operator
=	To assign value
+=	Adds two operands and assign a value to left operand
-=	Subtract two operands and assign a value to left operand
*=	Multiply two operands and assign a value to left operand
/=	Divide two operands and assign a value to left operand
%=	Divide two operands and assign remainder to left operand

Conditional operators

Conditional operators are also known as ternary operator.

Syntax

condition ? expression1 : expression2

If condition is true, expression1 is evaluated. If condition is false, expression2 is evaluated.

Bitwise Operators:

Bitwise operator works at bit level. Operations are converted into bits first and then calculations are performed. Mathematical operations like: addition, subtraction, addition and division are possible using bitwise operator. These operators are used for fast processing.

Operators	Meaning
&	Bitwise AND
|	Bitwise OR
^	Bitwise exclusive OR
~	Bitwise complement
<<	Shift left

The sizeof operator

sizeof operator gives the size in bytes. Sizeof operator needs one argument. The sizeof operator is used in a different ways like

Data type as an argument to sizeof operator

```
#include<stdio.h>
void main()
{
   printf("\n %d",sizeof(char));
   printf("\n %d",sizeof(int));
   getch();
}
```

Variable name as an argument to sizeof operator

It will print size of the variable according to the data type of that variable in bytes. If a variable type is float then it will return size of float data type.

```c
#include<stdio.h>
void main()
{
  int x;
    printf("\n %d",sizeof(x));
    getch();
}
```

Expression as an argument to sizeof operator

It will print size of the data type into which output will be generated. Here in example, answer of int value plus float value will be in float so this operator will give size of float in output. So we can say that a data type which occupies more bytes will come in output.

Example

```c
#include<stdio.h>
void main()
{
  int x;
  float y;
  printf("\n %d",sizeof(x+y));
```

```
    getch();
}
```

Variable

We are creating programs using specific language to do some task automatically. For that we need to store data into system and then system will do process on it and final output will be generated. To store user's data into computer we require memory space of a system that space is known as variable.

Note: Variable name
Must not start with a digit

Must not be a space

Must not be a keyword

Must be alphabets, digits and special characters like underscore (_) and dot(.)

Should be in lower case because c is case sensitive language.

Declaration of variables
Syntax :
        Data type variable name;

Example

```
int a;
float b,c;
```

There are two types of variable
- Local Variables
- Global Variables

Local Variables

A variable is a local if it is declared within any block. That block may be main () or UDF. We have to create a local variable on top of the block. The scope of the local variable is up to the execution of that block. It means we cannot get value of local variable outside of block. As an execution of a particular block will start local variable will be available and after execution it will die.

```
void main()
{
  int a=10;
    printf("\n a=%d",a);
  getch);
}
```

Global Variables

A variable is said to be a global if it is declared outside of all the functions in program. We can use global variable throughout the program. A global variable remains in the memory until the program terminates. Global variable is defined before main().

```
int a=10;
void val(void);

void main()
{
   printf("\n a=%d",a);
  getch);
}

void val(void)
{
   printf("\n a=%d",a);
}
```

Data Types in C
To store any data we require variable. That data should be of specific type which is known as data type. There are basic four types which are given below.

int - integer: used to store a whole number means without decimal point.

    Example: int a=10;

float - floating point value: used to store number with a fractional part.

    Example: float a=5.5;

double - used to store double value which has more capacity than float.

    Example: double a=5.7;

char - used to a single character.

    Example: char a='a';

Basic Structure of C Program

The general structure of C program is as shown below which we have to follow to develop any program using C.

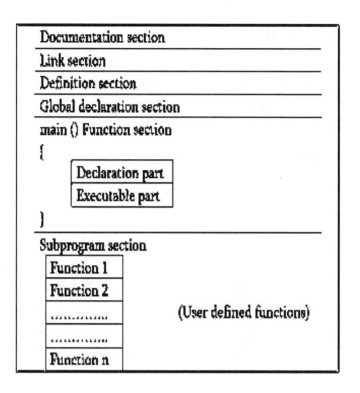

Documentation section: The documentation section will be always first in any program. We can include some information like definition of program, name of creator of program, date on which it is created etc.

Example

```
/*
   File name    : hello.c
   Author name  :
   Description  : program to display Hello
*/
```

Link section:

This section includes header file. The link section provides instructions to the compiler to link functions from the system library such as using the #include directive.

Example:

```
#include<stdio.h
```

Definition section:

The definition section defines all symbolic constants such using the #define directive. The #define is a preprocessor compiler directive which is used to create constants. We generally use uppercase letters to create constants. In the example code we have created a constant PI and assigned 3.1416 to it.

Example:

```
#define PI 3.14
```

Global declaration section:

Global means available for all. In a program we have main() and user defined functions. We may have variables which we would like to use in main() as well as in user defined functions. These types of variable we can declare before main(). We are declaring variables and user defined functions into global section.

Example:

> Int a;   // global variable declaration
> void msg(void);   // global function declaration
> (UDF)

main() section:

main() function is the heart of C program. Every C program must have one main function section. We can process some statements and make the logic of the program into this section. This section contains two parts; declaration part and executable part

1. **Declaration part:**

   We can declare variables which are used in executable part of a program.

2. **Executable part:**

main() is an executable part of the program. When {starts execution of the program will start. When }ends execution of the program will stop. We have to write at least one statement into the executable part of the program. As per the syntax, most of the statements are ends with semicolon (;).

> void main()
> {
>   printf("Hello");
> }

Subprogram section:

Sub program means user defined function. UDF is called from main(). UDF are used to perform a specific task.

Example

```
void msg(void)

    {

            printf("\n hello friends...");

    }
```

Practice

1. Print "Hello"
2. Print your bio-data with name, address, contact no, email id etc.
3. Input one value of an integer variable and print the same.
4. Input two values of an integer variable. Do arithmetic operations on it and print output.
5. Input two integer numbers and prints square and cube of it.
6. Calculate the area of circle.(PI * r * r)
7. Calculate simple interest.
8. Write a C program to enter marks of three subjects and calculate total, average and percentage.
9. Write a program to enter two numbers and swap that numbers.

Control Structure

Introduction:

Control structures are the structures used to control the flow of a program. There are two classification conditions and loops. In C, blocks means group of multiple statements together so they can be treated as one.

Types of control structures
1. Sequence
2. Selection
3. Repetition
4. Function call

Sequence:
Sequence means one by one in a specified order. We cannot omit any statement and even we cannot execute any statement more than once.

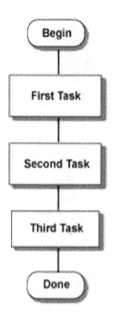

Example

```
#include<stdio.h>
void main()
{
        int a=5;
        printf("value of a = %d",a);
}
```

Selection:

Selection is possible from comparisons. When condition is true then selected statements will executed and when condition is false then another selected statements will be executed.

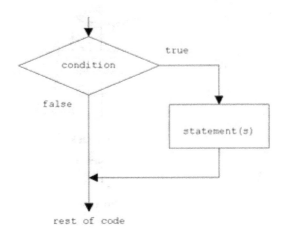

a. if statement-block

b. switch-case

if statement-block

If statement is also known as decision making statement. If statement is used to do comparison between two values or variables. We can define different conditions into our program if it is required. This block will return either true or false.

Different types of conditional statements

Simple if statement

If-Else statement

Nested If statement

Else If ladder

Simple if statement:

In a simple if, if a condition is true then block of statements will be executed otherwise we do not get any output.

Flowchart:

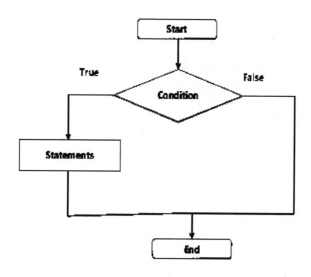

Syntax:

```
if (test-expression)
{
        statement-block;
}
```

Example

```
#include<stdio.h>
#include<conio.h>
void main()
{
int num=0;
clrscr();
        printf("enter the number");
        scanf("%d",&num);
                if(n%2==0)
                {
                        printf("%d number in even",num);
                }
  getch();
}
```

If-Else statement

The if-else statement is used to when we have comparison between two values. Here, if a condition is true then all statements inside true block will be executed. If a condition is false then all statements inside false or else block will be executed.

Flowchart:

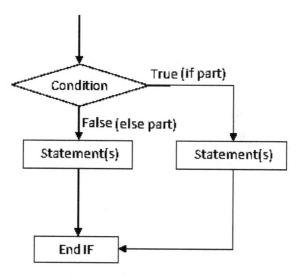

fig: Flowchart for if ... else statement

Syntax:

```
if(expression)
{
        //Statements;
}
else
{
        //Statements;
}
```

Example

```
#include<stdio.h>
#include<conio.h>
void main()
{
        int num=0;
        clrscr();
                printf("Enter the number --");
                scanf("%d",&num);

                if(n%2==0)
                {
                        printf("%d number in even", num);
                }
                else
                {
                        printf("%d number in odd",num);
                }
   getch();
}
```

Nested If
Nested means one into another. If is used to put condition and nested if is used to put condition into condition.

Flowchart:

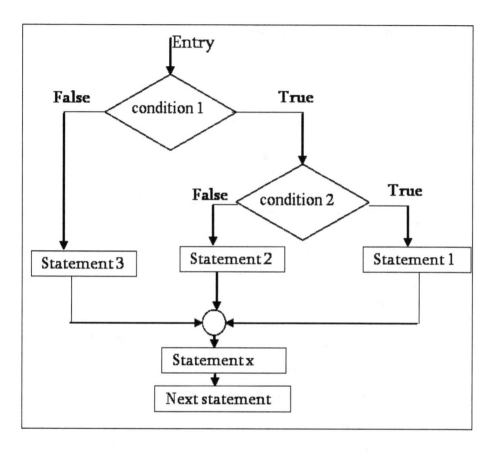

Syntax:

```
if (condition)
{
    if (condition)
    {
        statement-block;
```

```
            }

        else
        {
                statement-block;
        }
}
else
{
        statement-block;
}
```

Example
```c
#include<stdio.h>
#include<conio.h>
void main( )
{
  int a,b,c;
  clrscr();
  printf("Please Enter 3 number");
  scanf("%d%d%d",&a,&b,&c);
        if(a>b)
        {
                if(a>c)
                {
                        printf("a is greatest");
                }
```

```
            else
            {
                    printf("c is greatest");
            }
        }
        else
        {
            if(b>c)
            {
                    printf("b is greatest");
            }
            else
            {
                    printf("c is greatest");
            }
        }
        getch();
}
```

Else if ladder

When we have multiple conditions then this structure is useful. A first condition will always executed first. If first condition is false then control of the program transfers to the next condition.

Flowchart:

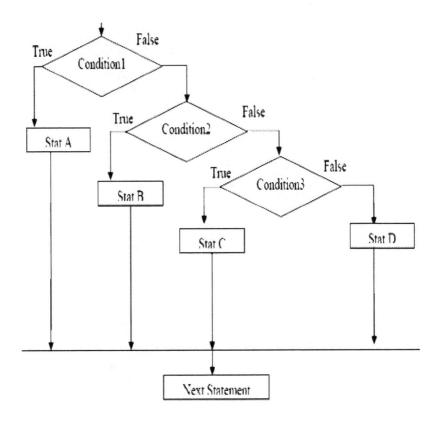

Syntax :

```
if(condition1)
{
        //statements;
}
else if(condition2)
{
        //statements;
}
```

38

```
        else
        {
                //statements;
        }
```

Example
```
void main( )
{
  int a;
  printf("Enter a number --");
  scanf("%d",&a);
        if( a%2==0 && a%4==0)
        {
                printf("divisible by both 2 and 4");
        }
        else if( a%2==0 )
        {
                printf("divisible by both 2");
        }
        else if( a%4==0 )
        {
                printf("divisible by both 4");
        }
        else
        {
                printf("not divisible by 2 and 4");
```

```
        }
        getch();
}
```

switch-case

Switch case statements are a substitute for long if
statements that compare a variable to several integral
values. A switch statement allows a variable to be tested for
equality against a list of values. Each value is called a case,
and the variable being switched on is checked for each
switch case. The switch statement is a multi branch
statement.

Points to remember

The variable provided into switch statement must have
constant value otherwise it would not be valid.

Case values should not be repeated.

No need to write default statement every time.

The break statement is used inside the switch to terminate a
statement sequence.

The break statement is optional. If omitted, execution will
continue on into the next case.

Nested switch structure is also possible like nested if.

You cannot use any condition with switch case.

A constant which is passed to switch must be of integer or character type.

We cannot use float data type with switch statement
You can use as many case as you wish within a switch.

Syntax:

```
switch(expression)
{
        case value-1:
                block-1;
                break;
        case value-2:
                block-2;
                break;

                ..........
                ..........

        default:
                Default-block;
                break;
}
```

Example:

```
#include<stdio.h>
```

```c
#include<conio.h>
void main()
{
        int ch;
        clrscr();
                printf("Enter any number (1 to 3)");
                scanf("%d",&ch);

        switch(ch)
        {
                case 1:
                        printf("your choice is 1");
                        break;
                case 2:
                         printf("your choice is 2");
                        break;
                case 3:
                        printf("your choice is 3");
                        break;
                default:
                        printf("Invalid choice");
        }
        getch();
}
```

Repetition OR Loop
Repetition means again and again but upto one condition.

It is also known as iteration or loop. It is used when a block of code needs to be executed several number of times. Loops are used when we need block of statements to be executed repeatedly until a condition is satisfied. There are three types of loops in C language that is given below:

a. do while

b. while

c. for

Flowchart

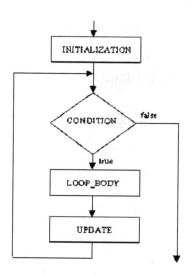

do...while loop

When we need that block of statements are executed at least once at that time do…while loop is used. This loop executes the body of the loop first and at last it will check the condition. If condition is true then again that block of statements will be executed else control will be passed next to the loop.

Syntax:

```
initialization;
do
{
        //code to be executed
}while(condition);
```

Example

```
#include<stdio.h>
#include<conio.h>
void main( )
{
   int i=1;
   clrscr();
   do
   {
       printf("\n %d",i);
       i++;
   }while(a<=10);
getch( );
}
```

While loop

While loop has one control condition, and executes as long the condition is true. The condition of the loop is tested

44

before the body of the loop is executed; hence it is called an entry-controlled loop.

Syntax

```
while (condition)
    {
        statement(s);
        increment / decrement;
    }
```

Example

```
#include<stdio.h>
#include<conio.h>
void main( )
{
   int i=1;
   clrscr();
   while(i<=10)
   {
       printf("\n %d",i);
       i++;
   }
getch( );
}
```

for loop

For loop is also known as open ended loop. In one statement we can write initialization, condition and increment/decrement in this loop.

Syntax:

for(initialization; condition; increment/decrement)
{
        //code to be executed
}

Here, two semicolons are used to differentiate initialization, condition and increment / decrement. Even we can use comma for multiple initialization or increment/decrement. We cannot write multiple conditions in for loop.

For loop is executed as follows:

It first evaluates the initialization code.

Then it checks the condition expression.

If it is true, it executes the for-loop body.

Then it evaluates the increment/decrement condition and again follows from step 2.

When the condition expression becomes false, it exits the loop.

Example

```
#include<stdio.h>
#include<conio.h>
void main()
{
        int i;
        clrscr();
        for(i=1;i<=5;i++)
        {
                printf("\n %d",i);
        }
        getch();
}
```

Jumping Statements

Jumping statements are used to transfer the program's control from one location to another; these are set of keywords which are responsible to transfer program's control within the same block or from one function to another.

There are four jumping statements in C language:
   a. goto statement
   b. break statement
   c. continue statement
   d. return statement

goto statement

The goto statement is one type of jumping statement which jumps from one statement to another statement in the same program. There is no requirement of condition when we are using goto statement but we have to give destination point in form of label with it.

Syntax:

goto label;

Example

```
#include<stdio.h>
void main()
{
        printf("\n Monday");
        printf("\n Tuesday");
        printf("\n Wednesday");
                goto hello;
        printf("\n Thrusday");
        printf("\n Friday");
        printf("\n Satday");

        hello:
        printf("\n Sunday");
    getch();
}
```

Break statement:

The break is a keyword which is used to stop a current process. This statement can be used with loop or switch statement. When compiler reaches at break statement then it will stops current process and jumps to the next step if any.

Example

```
#include<stdio.h>
void main()
{
   int i;
   for(i=1; i<=5; i++)
   {
      printf("%d ",i);
      if(i==3)
      {
         break;
      }
   }
}
```

Continue statement:

Continue is used to transfer the program's control at the beginning of the loop. It forces the next iteration of the loop to be executed.

Example

```c
#include<stdio.h>
void main()
{
  int i;
      for(i=1; i<=5; i++)
      {
              printf("%d ",i);
              if(i==3)
              {
                      continue;
              }
      }
}
```

return statement

return statement is used to transfer program's control from called function to calling function. Secondary task is to carry value from called function to calling function. The return statement ends the current function and returns control in previous function.

Example

```c
// function with no return type
      void myFun(void)
      {
              printf("Hello");
              return;
```

```
        printf("Hi");
   }
// will not print Hi
```

Practice

1. Input 2 numbers and print the maximum among them.
2. Input 2 numbers and print the minimum among them.
3. Input 3 numbers and print the maximum among them.
4. Input a number & print the number is odd or even.
5. Write a program to find whether the year is leap or not.
6. Input a number and check whether the number is positive, negative or zero.
7. Input cost price and selling price. Calculate profit or loss.
8. Input marks of three subjects. Calculate total, percentage and grade. Grades like distinction, first class, second class, pass or fail.
9. Input one character from the user. Check that character is vowel or consonant.
10. Display 1 to 10.
11. Display 10 to 1
12. Display 1,3,5,7,9,

13. Display 1,2,4,8,16,32,64,
14. Display 1,10,2,9,3,8,4,7,5,6,
15. Display sum of 1 to 10.
16. Input one integer no from user. Display reverse of it.
17. Input one integer no from user. Do sum of all digits of it.
18. Input one integer no from user. Calculate its factorial.
19. Input one integer no from user. Check that number is prime or not.
20. Input one integer no from user. Check that number is armstrong or not.
21. Input one integer no from user. Display fibonacci series upto that number. (0 1 1 2 3 5 8 ... n)
22. Print 1 to 10 using goto statement

Function

A function is a block of code that performs a specific task.

Functions can be divided into two categories

Library functions
User-defined functions

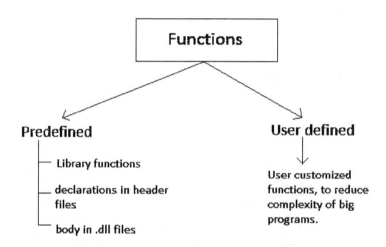

Library functions:

Library function means functions which are already available in the library of C language. Example printf(), scanf(), getch() etc. We have to just include appropriate header files to use these functions.

User Defined Functions (UDF)

UDF means a special block of statements which is created by user as per requirement. When some code is required more than once in a same program then user can create UDF and use that code again and again by calling that function.

Benefits

It divides a program in a small different bunches.

It provides reusability of code.

It provides easier way to find error in the program.

It makes program more logical.

Function Declaration

A function means UDF must declared before it is used in a program. Declaration of a function must be before main(). So a compiler came to know that which function, with how many arguments and will it return a value or not by its declaration. The actual code of the function may comes after main(). It is known as function prototyping.

Declaration of function
Syntax

returntype FunctionName(argument1, argument2, ...);

Returntype :

Return type specifies the type of value(int,float,char,double) that function is expected to return to the program which called the function.

Function name :
Function name specifies the name of the function.

Parameter list OR Arguments
The parameter list declares list of parameters with its data type. So a user has to pass that many arguments with the proper data type to the program.

Terminating with semicolon
A function name ends with semicolon. So a compiler should understand that here we have only declaration of a function is available. Detailed function will come later.

Calling a function
When a function is called from any function or main() then control of the program will transfer to the called function.

There can be 4 different types of user-defined functions, they are:

Function with no arguments and no return value

Function with arguments and no return value

Function with no arguments and a return value

Function with arguments and a return value

1. Function with no arguments and no return value

```
#include <stdio.h>
void msg();
void main()
{
    msg();   // no argument is passed to msg()
}
void msg()
{
        printf("\n Hello Friends...");
}
```

2. Function with arguments and no return value

```
#include <stdio.h>
void printVal(int);
void main()
{
    int a=10;
```

```c
        printVal(a);
    getch();
}
void printVal(int x)
{
    printf("\n x=%d",x);
}
```

3. Function with no arguments and a return value

```c
        #include <stdio.h>
        int printVal(void);
        void main()
        {
          int a;
            a=printVal();
                printf("\n a=%d",a);
            getch();
        }
        int printVal()
        {
```

```c
    int x=10;
    return x;
}
```

4. Function with arguments and a return value

```c
#include <stdio.h>
int printVal(int);
void main()
{
    int a=10,b;
    b=printVal(a);
        printf("\n b=%d",b);
    getch();
}
int printVal(int x)
{
    int y;
    y=x+5;
    return y;
}
```

Practice

1) Create a user define function named add which accepts 1 integer and 1 float values as an arguments and return the addition of it.

2) Create a user define function named sq which accepts 1 integer value as an arguments and return the square of it.

Arrays

To store any value we are using variable with a particular data type. But when we want to store more than one value of the same data type then we can use array. Each value of an array is also call element of an array. Size of the array must be a constant value. In short, array is a collection of variables belongs to same data type.

Types of an Array:

1. One Dimensional Array
2. Two Dimensional Array

One Dimensional Array:

One dimensional array has only one dimension means we can consider it either as a row or as a column. It stores values or elements one after another. It gives index to each element. Index starts with zero(0). It is also known as linear array.

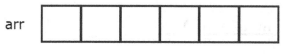

arr

an array of 6 elements

Syntax:

datatype array_name[size];

Example

```
#include <stdio.h>
void main()
{
    int a[5], i;
    for(i=0; i<5; i++)
    {
        printf("Enter value --- ");
        scanf("%d", &a[i]);
    }
    for(i=0; i<5; i++)
    {
        printf("\n %d: ",a[i]);
    }
  getch();
}
```

Two Dimensional Array:

Two dimensional array has two dimensions means we can consider it with rows and columns. When we are defining array at that time first argument is row and second is column.

Example

```
#include<stdio.h>
#include<conio.h>
void main()
{
    clrscr();
    int a[2][2],i, j;

    for(i=0; i<2; i++)
    {
        for(j=0; j<2; j++)
        {
            scanf("%d",&a[i][j]);
        }
    }
    for(i=0; i<2; i++)
    {
        for(j=0; j<2; j++)
        {
```

```
                    printf("%d",a[i][j]);
            }
                printf("\n");
        }
    getch();
}
```

Character Array

String is a set of characters. Last character is null character '\0' in any string. Null character indicates end of a string. There is no data type like string in a C language. A group of characters can form a string for that we require character array to store a string.

Example

The string "hello" contains 5 characters plus one more character null is automatically added at the end of the string which means total 6 characters are required. We cannot display null as a character.

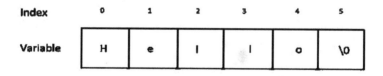

Index	0	1	2	3	4	5
Variable	H	e	l	l	o	\0

Declaring and initializing a character array
char str[10]={'L','e','s','s','o','n','\0'};

Example

```
#include <stdio.h>
void main ()
{
    char str[6] = {'H', 'e', 'l', 'l', 'o', '\0'};
    printf("\n Message : %s ",str);
}
```

Example

```
#include <stdio.h>
#include <conio.h>
void main()
{
    char str[20];
    printf("\n Enter a string :"); // string without space
    scanf("%s",str);
    printf("\n%s",str);
    getch();
}
```

Example:

```
#include <stdio.h>
#include <conio.h>
void main()
{
```

```
    char str[20];
    printf("\n Enter a string :"); // string with space
    gets("%s",str);
    puts("\n%s",str); // you can also use printf()
    getch();
}
```

Exercise

1. Input five integer numbers in an array. Display the same.

2. Input four integer numbers in 2D array.

3. Input five numbers in an array. Copy them in another array.

4. Input five numbers in an array. Find occurrence of first number from the array.

5. Input one string from the user. Check that string is palindrome or not.

6. Input five numbers in an array. Find maximum and minimum value from it.

7. Input five numbers in an array. Calculate average.

8. Input two 2X2 matrices from the user. Perform addition of it and print the output.

Structure and Union

Structure

A structure is a user defined data type in C. Structure is a collection of variables of different types under a single name. Struct keyword is used to declare a structure. A structure creates a data type that can be used to group items of possibly different types into a single type.

Structure is used to display a record type data. Suppose we want to keep record of employees. We might want to track attributes about each employee like empno, empname, salary etc.

Syntax:

```
struct structure_name
{
    data_type member1;
    data_type member2;
};
```

Note down:

You have to put semicolon at the end of the structure means after curly bracket [}].

Example

struct emp

```
{
    int empno;
    char empname[10];
};
```

Object Declaration

<u>Method 1:</u>
```
    struct emp
    {
        int empno;
        char empname[10];
    };

    void main()
    {
        struct emp e;
    }
```

<u>Method 2:</u>

```
    struct emp
    {
        int empno;
        char empname[10];
    }e;
```

Accessing members of a structure

67

We can use members of a structure by using dot operator(.)

Syntax:

object_name.member_name;

Example

```
#include<stdio.h>
struct emp
{
    int empno;
};

void main()
{
    struct emp e;
        printf("Enter employee no : ");
        scanf("%d",&e.empno);

        printf("\n\n Emplyee No = %d",e.no);
    getch();
}
```

Union

Unions are similar to structures in C. Union is a user defined data type. All members of union share the same memory location. Union allows storing of different data types. We have multiple members with different data type in a union like structure but only one variable can use allocated memory at a time. Union keyword is used to define a union.

Syntax:

```
union union_name
{
    data_type member1;
    data_type member2;
};
```

Example

```
union emp
{
    int empno;
    float salary;
};
```

Note down:

Here, total 4 bytes will be occupied in a memory. Either empno can be stored into that memory area or empname can be stored. In short, highest memory will be occupied.

Accessing members of a union

We can use members of a union like a member of a structure by using dot operator(.)

Syntax:

object_name.member_name;

Example 1:

```
#include<stdio.h>
union emp
{
    int empno;
};

void main()
{
    union emp e;
        printf("Enter employee no : ");
        scanf("%d",&e.empno);

        printf("\n\n Emplyee No = %d",e.no);
    getch();
}
```

Example 2:

```
#include<stdio.h>
union emp
{
    int empno;
```

```
      float salary;
   };

   void main()
   {
      union emp e;

          printf("Enter employee no : ");
          scanf("%d",&e.empno);
              printf("\n\n Emplyee No = %d",e.empno);

          printf("Enter salary : ");
          scanf("%f",&e.salary);
              printf("\n\n Emplyee Salary = %f",e.salary);

          getch();
   }
```

Practice

1. Create one structure with student as a name. Members
   of student structure are rno, mark1, mark2, tot and avg.
   All the members are of integer type. Input values of
   rno, mark1 and mark2 from the user. Calculate total and
   average. Print values of all members.

2. Create one structure with emp as a name. Members of
   emp structure are empno, basicsal, ta, da, hra, pf and

netsal. All the members are of integer type. Input values of empno and basicsal from the user. Calculate ta, da, hra, pf and netsal. Consider ta, da and hra as 5% of his/her basic salary. Pf is 10% of his/her basic salary. Print values of all members.